The Hungry Snowman
and Other Poems

The Hungry Snowman and Other Poems

by

Tina Tocco

Kelsay Books

© 2019 Tina Tocco. All rights reserved.
This material may not be reproduced in any form, published,
reprinted, recorded, performed, broadcast,
rewritten or redistributed without
the explicit permission of Tina Tocco.
All such actions are strictly prohibited by law.

Cover design by Shay Culligan

ISBN: 978-1-950462-04-9

Kelsay Books Inc.

kelsaybooks.com

502 S 1040 E, A119
American Fork, Utah 84003

To my mom~
My first editor,
who helps me with everything.

Acknowledgments

The author wishes to thank the editors and staff of the following publications and websites for initially publishing these poems (some in earlier versions):

Guideposts for Kids on the Web: "A Hundred Trees" (October 2002)

On the Line: "Leaves" (October 2004), "Waking" (March 2005)

Pockets: "When Raindrops Come Calling" (April 2004), "Holes in the Night" (June 2016), "Farewell, Fall" (November 2015)

Contents

Here Comes Spring

"Where Is Spring?"	13
Dreams	14
Spring Snow	15
Little Daisy	16
Waking	17
When Raindrops Come Calling	18
Afternoon in My Room	19

Summer Days, Summer Nights

Spring Vacation	23
What Makes Summer Best?	24
At the Plate	25
Holes in the Night	26
When the Sea	27
No!	28
Last of Summer	29

Time for Autumn

Autumn's Turn	33
A Hundred Trees	34
Leaves	35
Oh, to Be a Jack-o'-Lantern!	36
The Trees Look Down	37
"V"	38
Farewell, Fall	39

Winter Fun

Subject: Ready to Work?	43
Reply: Ready to Work?	44
Racing	45
Moonlight Skate	46
The Hungry Snowman	47
Snow Day	48
Night	49
Good-Bye, Skates	50
"Hey There, Spring!"	51

Here Comes Spring

"Where Is Spring?"

"Where is Spring?" gripes Winter,
pacing tall and straight.
"I've worked and worked for months now.
How dare she come home late!"

"I'm here!" calls Spring, a-running.
"I'm here to do my part.
So off to bed, my frosty friend.
It's time for me to start."

Dreams

Tulip, Tulip
do you dream
of sunlight, mist,
and coming Spring?

Spring, Spring
do you dream, too,
of sleeping petals
that dream of you?

Spring Snow

Spring snow, what a surprise!
I couldn't believe my sleepy eyes
when I woke this morning and you were here,
falling far and falling near.
Covering mountains, valleys, hills,
lawns and steps and windowsills.
Blowing over fields of green,
chimneys, roofs, our front porch screen.
Draping everything in white—
How did you sneak in overnight?
Although I dream of warmer days
with sticky heat and muggy haze,
you got it right—there is no doubt.
The roads are blocked—school is out!

Little Daisy

Little daisy,
do not hide.

Spring is here—
open wide!

Stretch your petals—
stand up tall!

You can sleep
in the fall.

Waking

Unfurled buds
Stiff, green
Coax the sun
Tease the rain
Whisper, "Wake me."

When Raindrops Come Calling

If three or four
or maybe more
raindrops came a-hollering
outside my old screen door
I think I'd say
I'd love to play
but could you drop by
another day
when I hadn't prepped
and planned and such
to munch
upon my picnic lunch?

Afternoon in My Room

Afternoon
in my room.
All day long
a hazy gloom.

All around
showers drown
an April day
while the windows pound.

That was the worst,
then sunshine's thirst
cracks the clouds
and dries the burst.

Windows wide!
Curtains fly!
A perfect day
to play outside!

Summer Days, Summer Nights

Spring Vacation

"Take off, Spring!" says Summer.
"You're not needed here.
"It's time for things to heat up!"
Spring smiles from ear to ear.

"That's fine with me," says Spring.
"I'm off to have some fun.
Have Winter call me next year
when my vacation's done."

What Makes Summer Best?

What makes summer best?
Is it just the hazy heat?
Is it spitting watermelon seeds
or getting sweaty feet?

Is it running through the sprinkler
as it shoots into the air?
Is it gazing up at clouds
to see what shapes are living there?

Is it leaping in a lake
where you can splash under the sun?
Is it knowing you have every day
to swing and jump and run?

Or is it laying in a field
where nothing makes a sound?
Or is it eating lunch and supper
on a blanket on the ground?

Or is it sleeping very late
and having time to rest?
What makes summer special?
What makes summer best?

At the Plate

Stiff as a post
I stand and wait
as the pitch zooms past
across home plate.

That's strike one.
Next time I swing.
The ball rockets past
with a *Zip!* and a *Zing!*

Last try now.
Steady…steady….
It's coming…it's coming….
This time, I'm ready.

Crack! goes the bat.
Whack! goes the ball.
Sailing…sailing….
over the wall!

The crowd cheers loud,
I grin and run
under the blazing
summer sun.

Holes in the Night

Lightning bugs
poke holes in the night
and fill them up
with bits of light.

But in the day,
where do they go?
With their lights off,
you'll never know!

When the Sea

When the sea
in a raging spree
growls and snaps
and chases me
I tell myself
it's just its way
of asking me
to come and play.

No!

There once was a boy named Clay,
who just wanted summer to stay.
Mother Nature said, "No!
Get ready for snow.
Cold weather is soon on its way."

Last of Summer

Slowly slip
our days of ease.
Autumn sneaks up,
starts to tease.

Rusting colors
ride the breeze.
Days turn shorter,
summer sleeps.

Time for Autumn

Autumn's Turn

Autumn's searching up and down—
Summer's hiding here.
It's sunny, hot, and sticky, too,
with flowers everywhere.

"There you are!" cries Autumn.
"Don't you ever learn?"
"Fine!" says Summer, hotly.
"You can have your turn."

A Hundred Trees

A hundred trees
in a forest glade
with a thousand boughs
to cast off shade
shed a million
rusted leaves
on a billion wisps of
autumn breeze
blown up high
tumbled low
rolled away
in a crinkly flow
curled up in a floaty pile
where I swing
                I jump
                        I fly
                              I smile.

Leaves

Tumbling, bumbling
Autumn leaves
Twirling, curling
In the breeze
Turning, churning
Coasting down
Piles and piles
Upon the ground

Oh, to Be a Jack-o'-Lantern!

Pick me! Pick me!
Can't you see?
I'm the best jack-o'-lantern
there will ever be!

Just carve me a frown
or a face like a clown,
but whatever you do,
don't put me down!

I'm the very best one.
I'll make Halloween fun.
I'll scare all the kids
'til they run, run, run!

I know that I'm small
and shaped like a ball.
Hey, give me a chance.
I'll give it my all!

We're going away?
You're making my day!
Front porch—here I come
to scare kids away!

I knew you'd pick me.
I knew that you'd see.
I'm the best jack-o'-lantern
there will ever be!

The Trees Look Down

The trees look down
upon the ground.
They shake their heads
and sigh.

But when they shake
their colors flake
and Autumn
waves good-bye.

"V"

Winter's coming.
How do you know?
The geese are flying high.

A "V" of feathers
streaks itself
across a sunset sky.

Deep and low
their honks call out.
"Too cold for us!" they bellow.

They leave us
in our autumn chill
for weather warm and mellow.

Farewell, Fall

Leaves
    Breeze
        Changing trees
            Whipping winds
                Colder eves
                    Early snows
                        Nipping nose
                            Winter's coming
                                Autumn goes.

Winter Fun

Subject: Ready to Work?

Hello, Old Man Winter,
I hope this finds you well.
Are you ready to wake up now
after your year-long sleeping spell?

Reply: Ready to Work?

Yes, I'm ready.
Go to sleep.
It's time for a cold stretch,
long and deep.

Racing

One flake falling!
Another swirls!
This one's skidding!
That one whirls!
Racing, racing—
not one sound.
Future snowmen
on the ground.

Moonlight Skate

Moonlight bathes
the lake with light.

Stars wink and blink
from a distant height.

Daddy's hands
hold mine tight

sliding, gliding
across the night.

The Hungry Snowman

There once was a hungry snowman
who fried icicles up in a pan.
When they melted away,
what could he say?
He needed a new dinner plan.

Snow Day

I pull on socks,
one pair, then two.

Next comes my sweater,
thick and blue.

Long underwear
to keep me snug.

Wooly pants
go up with a tug.

I snuggle my hat
atop my head.

Then bundle tight
in a scarf of red.

My boots rise up
to my knobbly knees.

My gloves go on
so my hands don't freeze.

What else? What else?
I think I'm done.

Snow day! Snow day!
Here I come!

Night

The field is a sea of endless white
washed with a mist of blue moonlight.
The hoof prints of a little doe
crack the freshly fallen snow.
Her mother's prints are just nearby—
two trails as quiet as the sky.
An owl hoots from a far-off height
as they wander free throughout the night.

Good-Bye, Skates

Last night, my skates ran away.
Their text had little to say.
"We need a vacation!"
it said in frustration.
"We won't be back until May."

"Hey There, Spring!"

"Hey there, Spring!" says Winter.
"It's wakey-wakey time.
I've got my PJs buttoned up
and my blanket's pulled up high."

"Thank goodness!" Spring says, all lit up.
"I'm bored stiff, anyhow.
So take a nap, my frosty friend.
I'll be in charge for now."

About the Author

Tina Tocco's work has appeared or is pending in many children's magazines, including *Highlights for Children, Highlights High Five, Cricket, Spider, AppleSeeds, Odyssey, Humpty Dumpty, Turtle,* and *Pockets*. Tina is a longtime member of the Society of Children's Book Writers and Illustrators, which awarded her an Honor Award in Poetry. She earned an MFA in creative writing from Manhattanville College.

www.ingramcontent.com/pod-product-compliance
Lightning Source LLC
LaVergne TN
LVHW091321080426
835510LV00007B/585